A SKETCH

OF

THE WATERLOO CAMPAIGN.

PREFACE.

THE difficulty of the student contemplating the study of Military History is that, amid the vastness of the material available, he is apt to find himself at a loss to know where to make a beginning. It is with the object of meeting this, and assisting him at the outset, that the following pages on the Waterloo Campaign have been written. I have endeavoured as concisely as possible, yet without omitting anything of importance, to record the events which preluded the final climax at Waterloo, and it is my hope that the account I have given may introduce the student to a knowledge of the art of war and induce him to pursue it with pleasure and profit for its own sake. This seems to me the more desirable, as acquaintance with Military History is now being insisted upon as a necessary part of an officer's professional equipment.

SEYMOUR CLARKE.

Inverness,
    December, 1903.

CONTENTS.

A SKETCH

OF

THE WATERLOO CAMPAIGN.

CHAPTER I.

" No kind of history so fascinates mankind as the history of wars. No kind of record, other than sacred, appeals at once to the deep sympathies of so wide an audience "—so writes Sir Edward Hamley in his admirable work " The Operations of War." And I really think no one can doubt the truth of the above assertion.

When our great nation is engaged in a campaign one has only to observe how quickly the morning papers are bought up and eagerly read to prove, if proof is necessary, that soldier and civilian alike take a deep interest in the " history of wars."

To understand Military History aright we must study the campaigns and battles of the great captains that have gone before, and take note of how they acted both when victorious and when defeated. All great soldiers of note read Military History, and read

B

deeply—Turenne, Frederick the Great, Napoleon, and Von Moltke, we are told, studied deeply and constantly the art of war; and our great Duke of Wellington made it a rule to study for some hours every day.

The military student is often afraid to approach the vast amount of literature concerned in order to accomplish his end, and may be he thinks that Military History is dry and dull and only to be attempted by those who are aspirants for Staff employment, and quite outside the province of the regimental officer.

But let him seriously study one campaign, and he will find in it so much of interest that his eyes will be opened, and he will look upon Military History from a totally different point of view—a new vista of ideas will suddenly appear on his horizon.

However, let us suppose that the student has determined that he will read Military History. The question arises where is he to begin? My answer to that question would be let him commence with the Waterloo Campaign, so glorious to the British Army.

By Waterloo Campaign I mean to include from the 14th till 18th June, 1815.

"Napoleon left Paris on June 12th for the Valley of the Sambre, and was back there again on the 21st as a fallen and defeated monarch."—(Lord Wolseley).

In this campaign the student will read of three

battles, and study the dispositions made by three great captains—Wellington, Blücher, and Napoleon.

He will understand how the face of Europe might have been altered had Napoleon been victorious at Waterloo, and what an enormous stake the Emperor fought for on that memorable day, the 18th June; he will realise the military genius of the great Duke of Wellington and the noble co-operation of the Prussians under the magnificent Prince Blücher; he will be able to argue with himself what the result to the allies would have been had Napoleon's health not broken down on the 16th of June, also had D'Erlon's Corps acted as the Emperor intended on this day.

Again, had Grouchy pursued the retreating Prussians *at once* after the Battle of Ligny, when he himself wanted to do so, but could get no instructions from Napoleon owing to the latter's temporary illness; and again, had that same general marched " to the sound of the cannon " on the 18th and crossed the Dyle, he could ask himself would all have gone well with the allies during this campaign. And perhaps the greatest question he could ask himself : had Prince Blücher retired on his own base—Cologne, via Namur and Liege—as many leaders would have done under the circumstances, would Waterloo have been fought at all? These are only a few of the questions the military student might put to himself; others will suggest themselves to him as he pursues the subject.

The scene of the Waterloo Campaign is laid in Belgium—the country lying between the Sambre River, in the south, and Antwerp, in the north. The country of Belgium is much intersected by roads and canals; there are more roads in Belgium, and they are better kept, than in any other country in Europe, with the exception of Great Britain.

Belgium is in the shape of a triangle, with its base resting on France. The length of this base is about 380 miles; its area is, roughly, twice the area of the county of Yorkshire. Looking at the map, it will be seen that the tendency of the rivers is to flow northwards, which indicates that the country slopes from south to north. It also dips from east to west. The highest land is on the east; on the west it is below the level of the sea, the German Ocean being kept out by dykes and sand-dunes some 50 feet high; the length of the coast line, roughly, measures 40 miles.

On the whole Belgium is a flat country; in fact, the north of the country is part of the great Plain of Europe, while the country in the south-east is the plateau of Ardennes, of which the highest point is Stavelot, over 2,000 feet high.

There is also the region of Peel and Campine in the north-east, with marsh, bog, and sand, overgrown with heath and fir, and quite sterile, which is in marked contrast to the rest of Belgium, which is, for the most part, very well cultivated and covered with rich vegetation.

Here I would recommend the student, before beginning to study a campaign, to glance through a geography, with an atlas in front of him, so as to get the general lie of the country into his mind.

The climate of Belgium is very similar to that of the South of England, but the extremes of heat and cold are greater. The annual rainfall is about 28 inches in the west, but is greater in the east.

I think it right to dwell on the general topography and the climate of the theatre of war, as so much hinges upon both of them.

Without good maps the commander of an army works in the dark, hence the communications, *i.e.*, railways, canals, roads, and the general surface of the country, are of first moment to him; and again the climate, when we consider the great differences that climate makes to an army in the field. Take, for example, the retreat from Moscow of Napoleon's Army in the bitter winter of 1812, when the thermometer registered 30 degrees below zero on the 6th December —the greatest instance of the effect of climate recorded in history.

Excessive rainfall seriously affects the marching powers of an army, and, remembering the state of the roads on the 17th and 18th of June, 1815, owing to the abnormal amount of rain that fell on the first-mentioned day, and how it influenced the troops engaged, particularly the Prussians, who experienced difficulties in bringing their guns into action on the 18th, and Napoleon's delay in commencing the Battle of Waterloo, the importance of these factors will not surprise the military student. It may be taken as a rough guide that five minutes must be added to the ordinary time of traversing a mile of road in heavy rain over muddy roads ; and ten minutes must be added for troops to traverse a stretch of hilly country road.

The map of the theatre of war, which I offer to my readers, is only intended to be rough, but, it being on a fairly large scale, viz., about 3 miles to 1 inch, the roads will, I hope, show clearly the routes taken by the principal actors in this great campaign.

With a small map one is apt not to appreciate sufficiently the distance from place to place. Thus one is in danger of getting a false idea of time and space and of the difficulties of moving troops within a given period.

I would recommend to the military student, when investigating a map of any theatre of war, to cut for himself a long strip of cardboard, or drawing paper, and carefully tick off from the scale supplied with the map the various distances marked thereon, letting the strip be sufficiently long to take in the limits of the whole map, and not merely a few miles, as the scale on the plan shows. This is an infinitely better method than using the dividers or compasses, as both the latter injure the face of the map to a certain extent ; besides, this method, in my opinion, is the quicker in the end.

I have shown on the right and left hand top corners of the map the general directions of the bases of the Prussian and British commanders, in order to bring it home to the student how very important the base and the lines of communication are to an army in the field.

Every commander jealously watches his lines of communication, and justly so ; if cut off from them, how is his army to be fed, clothed, and, of such vast importance, how is it to be shod ? And of equal importance, how is ammunition to be brought to the front ; how are the wounded to be sent to the rear ?

With reference to this campaign, as regards the two bases of the allied British and Prussian armies, I would ask the reader for a moment to glance at the map of Belgium and Germany. He will see, roughly speaking—taking the line Quatre-Bras-Sombref as the starting point—that Antwerp and Ostend (Wellington's base), and Cologne (Blücher's base), are almost at right angles to each other.

Now what would have happened (and really what Napoleon hoped and expected would happen) had Blücher retired on Cologne, his base, and Wellington on either Antwerp or Ostend ? The answer is simple ;

the Allies would have been divided, and Napoleon would only have had to deal with each army in detail, and, as he was superior in numbers to each separately, the chances of victory would have been all in his favour.   Further, it must be granted that Napoleon was a greater tactician than Blücher, and, taking into consideration that our great Duke's force was a heterogeneous one, consisting of many nations, less than one-third being British ; while on the other hand Napoleon's army was composed entirely of French-men, and had many Peninsular veterans in the ranks, we must allow that Napoleon had decidedly the advantage.

To Blücher, and Blücher alone, is the credit due for retiring to the northward, and not to the eastward, viz., towards the Prussian base, after Ligny.

I allow that Gneisenau, the chief of the Prus-sian staff—fine tactician as he was—gave the route to the north, *i.e.*, to WAVRE, after Blücher was unhorsed and *hors-de-combat*, but that was only because Tilly, which he at first had indicated, was not marked on the maps used by the Prussian staff.

Gneisenau, as is well-known, distrusted Wellington, and thought he had not done all he could at Ligny to help the Prussians, but how could he ? He had as much as he could do to stave off Ney's attack at Quatre-Bras, and thus could not co-operate as he had promised.   But this promise which was made to

Blücher, near a windmill, between Ligny and Brye, had the proviso—if he himself *was not seriously attacked.* The hour the Duke promised to come to Blücher's assistance was 4 p.m.

Fortunately for Europe Blücher was none the worse of his accident, and was again in the field in time to take command previous to the final issue. The Prussian army (three corps) retreated on WAVRE, two of them viâ Tilly and Gentinnes, and the third viâ Gembloux, the latter joined by Bülow's Corps (the 4th), coming up from Liege ; and all encamped on the night of the 17th June in the vicinity of WAVRE. And how nobly they came into the fray the next day at Waterloo! Bülow's Corps, which was the freshest, not having been engaged at Ligny, appeared on the battlefield at about 5 p.m., by the southern road, viâ St. Lambert and Lasne, and Ziethen's Corps at 7 p.m., by the northern road, viâ Ohain. These were followed by Pirch's Corps, which came by the same road as Bülow's Corps, at 7 p.m. Bülow's Corps moved on the French right at Planchenoit, Ziethen's Corps joined Wellington's left at Frishermont, and Pirch's Corps was directed on Maransart.

CHAPTER II.

I have endeavoured, imperfectly, I fear, to roughly locate on the map the positions of the belligerents from the 14th to 16th June. I have purposely avoided placing the troops on the map on the 18th—the day of the great contest at Waterloo—first because the map would have been so over-crowded and scarce intelligible, that a larger scale map of the neighbourhood round the country, south of the Soignes Forest, would have been necessary. A further reason is this, that in Sir Edward Hamley's "Operations of War," the "Story of Waterloo," by Colonel H. D. Hutchinson, and "Deeds that Won the Empire," by the Rev. W. H. Fitchett, the student can find for himself most excellent plans of the great battle.

14TH JUNE.—FRENCH.

With regard to this map of mine I have tried to show the French army—

(a) Gérard's Corps, which moved up from the Moselle, i.e., from the south-east, almost reaching Philippeville, on the 14th June.

(b) The Corps of Vandamme, Lobau, and the Imperial Guard, which arrived at Beaumont on the

14th; and here Napoleon himself established his head-quarters for the night of the 14th.

(*c*) Reille's and D'Erlon's Corps, which also arrived on the 14th June at Solre-sur-Sambre.

The French army, having closed in towards its centre from the line Lille-Metz, it will be seen that Napoleon has thus telescoped his force from a frontage of some 250 miles to one of less than 20 miles. I would here advise the student to study the map of the north-east of France and the Belgium frontier; and let him note the marked contrast in the case of the Allies, who on this date had a frontage of 100 miles by 40 deep.

It will be observed that all three places, viz., Philippeville, Beaumont, and Solre, are about equi-distant from CHARLEROI, roughly speaking, 16 to 18 miles—which was the main point where Napoleon intended to cross the Sambre; thus we see the clever concentration of the French army under Napoleon—the great strategist.

14TH JUNE.—PRUSSIANS.

On this day the Prussian headquarters were at Namur, the only corps opposed to the French Emperor being Ziethen's Corps of 30,000 men at Charleroi. The other three available were Pirch's, at Namur, Thielemann's at Ciney, and Bülow's at Liege,

far distant.   Brigades supplied by Ziethen's Corps
were stationed along the Sambre to watch the enemy,
and continued to the west by the Dutch-Belgians
from Nivelles.   The vedettes of the Prussians were
pushed to the south of the Sambre, and connected
with the Dutch-Belgian cavalry beyond Mons.

I have marked these troops, as far as possible, on
the map.

14TH JUNE—BRITISH.

The headquarters of the British army were at
Brussels.   The army consisted of two corps, a reserve,
and a corps of cavalry.   The first corps, under
the Prince of Orange, was at Mons, Enghien, and
Nivelles.   The second, under Lord Hill, was further
to the west, as far as the rivers Scheldt and Lys.
The cavalry were under Lord Uxbridge, and to him
was attached the German Legion.   The reserves were
in and around Brussels.   Here the student must refer
to the map of Belgium, as the above-named places are
not all included in my map.

15TH JUNE—FRENCH.

The French army, moving in three columns, started
before daylight on this day—

(*a*) Gérard's Corps, from Philippeville to Chatelet,
on the right.

(*b*) The Corps of Vandamme, Lobau, and the Guard from Beaumont to Charleroi, in the centre.

(*c*) The Corps of Reille and D'Erlon, from Solre-sur-Sambre to Marchiennes, on the left.

The Prussians, who held the bridges at Marchiennes, Charleroi, and Chatelet, were driven in by the French. Ziethen neglected to destroy these bridges before retreating—a very great tactical error. It will be noticed that Napoleon has again telescoped his frontage, which this morning was from Solre to Philippeville. It is now only from Marchiennes to Chatelet, about six miles—a magnificent example of concentration.

15TH JUNE—PRUSSIANS.

Except for Ziethen's error in not destroying the above-mentioned bridges, his tactics were otherwise sound. He fell back fighting in perfect order, his advance brigades closing in on their centres and joining hands to the north of Fleurus. In the meantime Pirch's Corps, from Namur, was moving up the Namur-Sombref road, and reached Mazy this day, which is about six miles from Ligny. Thielemann's Corps was also moving from Ciney, and reached Namur this day. Bülow, who was at Liege, and had evidently not fully understood Gneisenau's order to concentrate rapidly, was moving, but not rapidly enough for the occasion.

15TH JUNE—BRITISH.

On this day Wellington's outposts were pushed back by Ney, who moved on Frasne, viâ Gosselies, but the latter did not proceed further, and occupied Frasne for the night. The reader might take note here of the want of activity on the part of Ney. Ney seems to have served his master in a half-hearted manner since the latter's return from Elba, and showed little of that brilliancy which he had exhibited in previous campaigns, notably, the masterly way he handled the rear-guard in the Retreat from Moscow in 1812.

Wellington, at Brussels, had heard of the French being in motion to the south of the Sambre, but was of the opinion it was only a feint on their part—in fact, he still believed that Napoleon intended to make his attack on the British right, *i.e.*, from Lille, between the rivers Scheldt and Lys, and endeavour to cut off his (Wellington's) lines of communication with Ostend. And thus not one unit of the British army was moved on this day, so its position was identically the same as on the 14th. (*Vide* Note 2, end of book.)

As soon as Wellington was convinced that it was no feint on the part of the French, his orders were quickly written, and were issued before 5 p.m. The orders that most interest us are (1) "the Fifth Division, 81st Regiment, and Hanoverian Brigade of the Sixth Division, to be ready to march from Brussels at a moment's notice." (2) " Duke of Brunswick's Corps to collect this night on the road between Brussels and Vilvorde."

N.B.—Vilvorde is 6 miles N.N.E. of Brussels.

CHAPTER III.

16TH JUNE—BATTLE OF LIGNY—FRENCH v. PRUSSIANS.

The Battle of Ligny began at about 2.30 p.m. by the two French corps, viz., Vandamme's and Gérard's, which had been assigned to Grouchy, together with three corps of reserve cavalry, against the Prussians, consisting of Ziethen's Corps, Pirch's Corps (which had arrived at 6 a.m.), and Thielemann's, which also had arrived at noon, in addition to 224 guns. Lobau's Corps came to the support of the French at 5.30 p.m.

Napoleon was under the impression that only Ziethen's Corps was in position to oppose him, and this seems strange, as Napoleon, according to his custom, had made a reconnaissance, *in person*, of the Prussian position. (*Vide* " Combined Training," 1902, para. 10 (2).) Here the student might compare with advantage the activity displayed by the Emperor in his reconnaissance *in person* of the enemy's position, which is so essential to a commander in the field, with his lethargy on the 18th, when he failed to reconnoitre Wellington's position at Waterloo.

When, however, the Emperor had discovered his mistake he sent a message to Ney to send him D'Erlon's Corps at once ; and, by an extraordinary coincidence, D'Erlon's Corps did move in the direction of St. Amand, but by no order of Ney's—who required D'Erlon badly.

D'Erlon was approaching Frasne, when the galloper carrying Napoleon's order to Ney, showed it to D'Erlon, with the result that the latter did turn off his corps to the right, and moved in the direction of Ligny.

Vandamme, on seeing this corps approaching, was mystified, and imagined it was the enemy breaking through ; as soon, however, as Napoleon grasped the fact that it was the long-looked-for support, he launched his reserves on the Prussians and drove them back. The Prussians, however, retreated in good order. The pursuit by the French was not taken up *at once*, and the latter failed to gather the full fruits of victory.

The student ought to take special notice of the movement of D'Erlon's Corps, as so much—so very much—depended on it this day. This corps took no active part in the Battle of Ligny, but morally it did, as Napoleon was able to thrust his reserves on the Prussians at the critical moment ; but on the other hand, had Ney had it with him, as he was entitled, this corps having been assigned to him, together with

c

Reille's, on the 15th June, by Napoleon himself, would
Wellington have been able to hold his own at Quatre-
Bras?

I have placed the troops on the map as far as
possible.

16TH JUNE—BATTLE OF QUATRE-BRAS—BRITISH v. FRENCH.

At Quatre-Bras the only force at first to oppose the
French was Perponcher's Dutch-Belgians of about
10,000 men. This general had taken upon himself
to assemble the brigades of his division at Quatre-
Bras instead of at Nivelles.

Ney's attack did not come on till 2 p.m.—an
unexpected delay, and fatal to the French.

Ney had only two divisions of infantry (of Reille's
Corps) and Piré's cavalry with which to make his first
assault, but at 3 p.m. he was joined by Prince Jerome's
division (of the same corps); the 4th Division
(Girard's,* also of this corps), was deflected to the
right, evidently with the intention of watching the
Prussians at Ligny.

Wellington had arrived at Quatre-Bras about 11.30
a.m., and was satisfied with the dispositions made
there. Suggesting some slight alterations, he then
rode off to converse with Blücher, and saw the
Prussian position at Ligny. He apparently was not

---

* Not to be confused with Gérard, who commanded a corps.

of the opinion that the Prussian commander had made the most of the ground at his disposal, as he was firmly convinced that Napoleon would have an easy task to overthrow the Prussians.

The Dutch-Belgians, under Perponcher, were reinforced, at about 3 p.m., by Picton's famous Fifth Division (see Note 5 at end of book), and later by the Brunswickers; and again, at 5 p.m., by Halkett's brigade from Braine-le-Comte, also by Kielmansegge's Hanoverian brigade, with two field batteries. All that came to Ney were some divisions of Kellermann's heavy cavalry. It was at this stage that Ney wanted D'Erlon's Corps so badly, and sent for him to move in his direction without delay. D'Erlon was just deploying his corps in the vicinity of Ligny when he received Ney's order, and immediately closed up to move back to Quatre-Bras. His troops were, however, tired out, and only arrived in front of the latter place in time to be of no use whatever, Ney having in the meantime withdrawn from the uneven contest; Wellington had received further reinforcements, including the 1st British Division from Enghien, with 12 guns. These last reinforcements arrived between 6 and 7 o'clock, bringing the Duke's force up to 30,000 infantry, 2,000 cavalry, and 68 guns, against the French, who had about 21,000 in the field.

No doubt Ney was chagrined at both D'Erlon and Napoleon, and this must account in a great measure for his inactivity the following day.

The above troops I have endeavoured to show, as far as possible, on the map.

17TH JUNE—FRENCH.

The supineness of the French army on this day must be put down to the want of energy on the part of the great Napoleon.   Lord Wolseley assigns this want of energy to some peculiar malady to which the Emperor was prone.   Whatever was the reason the fate of France hung in the balance, and it would seem that the Divine Providence had ordained that this disturber of the peace of Europe should disturb that continent no longer.

NIGHT OF 16TH AND 17TH JUNE AND DAY OF 17TH—BRITISH.

Wellington, on the night of the Battle of Quatre-Bras, slept at Genappe, and was unaware of how the Prussians had fared at Ligny.   He was early in the field the next morning, and heard from his own staff that Blücher had been overthrown the day previously, The messenger that the Prussian commander had sent having been wounded, he thus received no direct communication from Blücher.   Wellington could also see for himself Ney's force still in position in his front, which implied that the Prussians must have had the worst of the previous day's fighting.

Wellington, thus finding his left flank uncovered, had to retire on Waterloo, but in perfect order, and in no hurry whatever, Ney not taking advantage of the situation. Wellington's retirement was only once interrupted by some cavalry at Genappe, who were easily repulsed by Lord Uxbridge with the 1st Life Guards. The Duke draws attention to this engagement in his despatch.

When Wellington heard of Blücher's retirement he sent the latter information that he would halt to the south of the Soignes Forest and accept battle from Napoleon if he (Blücher) would send one or two corps to co-operate with him.

NIGHT OF 16TH AND DAY OF 17TH JUNE— PRUSSIANS.

(*a*) On the night of the 16th-17th June Ziethen's Corps retired by Tilly, and continued to march on the day of the 17th by Mont St. Guibert on WAVRE.

(*b*) On the same night Pirch's Corps retired by Gentinnes, and continued to march on the day of the 17th, also by Mont St. Guibert, on WAVRE.

(*c*) Thielemann's Corps, which covered the retreat, retired this night on Gembloux, and next day (the 17th) connected with Bülow's Corps coming up from Liege, and both retired on WAVRE, moving viâ Sart-les-Walhain, Bülow's Corps leading.

We might for a moment turn to the overthrow of
the Prussians at Ligny and the failure of the French
to follow up their victory by a vigorous pursuit.   The
blame of this inertness on the part of the French rests
entirely with Napoleon himself.   Grouchy, whom
Lord Wolseley describes as a second-rate general,
was anxious to pursue at once, but could get no
definite answer from Napoleon, and thus valuable
time slipped away, the Prussians in the meantime
retreating unmolested, and, as already stated, in good
order.

When the pursuit was eventually taken up by
Grouchy, with 33,000 men and 96 guns, at 2 p.m. on the
17th, the French did not even know in what direction
the enemy had retired—this seems to have been the
fault of Pajol's cavalry—but, *presuming* the enemy
must have made for their own base, *i.e.*, Cologne, viâ
Liege, Grouchy followed, and only got as far as
Gembloux, torrents of rain impeding his march, and
he arrived there at 9 p.m., long after the Prussians had
left.

Grouchy has been censured for his action on this
occasion, and again on the 18th, for not marching to
the " sound of the cannon," but this is outside our
province to discuss.   All I want to bring out is that
when victorious in an action, pursue *at once* with *all*
your available force, and turn what is *merely* a victory
into a rout of the enemy.   This is a tactical principle

which must not be lost sight of by the military student. Our "Combined Training, 1902," para. 21, is very emphatic on this point, which the student would do well to study. While observing the neglect on the part of the French to pursue, I would draw special attention, and in marked contrast to it, how the Prussians followed up the French after the Battle of Waterloo.

To the student who desires to read of the charges against Grouchy, I refer him to the "Operations of War," pages 196—198.

NIGHT OF 17TH-18TH JUNE.

We know that Wellington retired from Quatre-Bras on Waterloo on the day of the 17th, undisturbed by the enemy, with exception of the cavalry action at Genappe, but not undisturbed by the elements. A fierce storm of rain and thunder raged, and the *British* army reached its destination drenched to the skin, and lay down to rest on the ground (within a mile of the enemy), where they were to fight on the morrow the great Battle of Waterloo.

The Prussians were in and about WAVRE on the night of 17th-18th June. The corps of Ziethen and a part of Thielemann's only were across the river Dyle. It might be asked why the Prussians did not make for a more direct route to Waterloo, *i.e.*, viâ

Mousty, or by a road further to the south.   The
answer to this is these roads were impracticable owing
to the marshy state of the country roads caused by
the recent rains.   *The French*, under Ney, on the
afternoon of 17th, were following Wellington up the
Charleroi-Brussels road, the Emperor, with Lobau's
Corps, the Guard anu reserve cavalry, joined Ney
coming from Marbais.   Napoleon's force at this time
amounted to about 72,000 men and 246 guns.

CHAPTER IV.

I do not want to dwell on the great and glorious victory at Waterloo, so many graphic descriptions of it being extant and accessible to the student ; besides, it would be presumptuous of me to try and make this mighty battle clearer to him.   I would simply draw attention to a few points—

(1) The lateness of the hour that Napoleon began the contest, viz., 11.50 a.m.   The reason given for this is that owing to the terrible rains that fell on the 17th, and continued unceasingly till the early hours of the morning of 18th, the ground had become so soft that it made the movement of artillery most difficult. Here the student will observe the fatal mistake Napoleon made.   Had he attacked at dawn, or soon afterwards, in spite of the softness of the ground, he might possibly have overwhelmed Wellington before Blücher had time to come up.

(2) I have already referred to the gallant co-operation of the Prussians, with Bülow's Corps arriving at 5 p.m., viâ St. Lambert, and Ziethen's Corps at 7 p.m., viâ Ohain ; so it is perhaps needless to again revert to it, but, as the result of the Battle of Waterloo hung so much upon Prussian support, it would be an omission on my part not to mention it in this place.

(3) Grouchy, with his 33,000 men, and near 100 guns, was absent ; his neglect to march to the " sound of the cannon " is a much vexed question.   I have already referred to it, and told the reader where he can find the argument for and against Grouchy's action for himself.   The enormous difference the absence of this corps made to Napoleon is evident to the most casual reader.

(4) Further, I would suggest to the student that the Battle of Waterloo might be conveniently considered under the following headings : —

(*a*) The attack on Hougoumont by Reille's Corps at 11.30 a.m. (secondary attack).

(*b*) The attack on the British left centre and centre by D'Erlon's Corps, supported by 78 guns, at 1.30 p.m. (main attack).

(*c*) The latter attack driven back by Picton's famous 5th Division and Ponsonby's and Somerset's cavalry.

(*d*) The magnificent, but fruitless, charges (said to be 13 in number) of the French cavalry.

(*e*) The assault on La Haye Sainte by Ney's infantry.

(*f*) The Prussian co-operation.

(*g*) Lobau's Corps detached to oppose the Prussian advance.

(*h*) The attack by the Imperial Guard.

(*i*) Grouchy's failure to be present at the battle.

(*j*) Flight of the Emperor and dispersion of the French army.

(*k*) The Prussian pursuit.

N.B.—In actual numbers, until the arrival of the Prussians, the opposing hosts were almost equal, except in guns, the French having 246 to Wellington's 156, a majority of 90 guns in favour of the French, a vast advantage. It must be remembered that Wellington had 18,000 men at HAL.

I have attempted in this short account to put this most interesting campaign, up to the crowning victory of Waterloo, in as clear a light as possible. As I said at the outset, it is the one, in my opinion, best suited to give the student his first insight into Military History—" the shortest and one of the most decisive in our history."

I am well aware of the many shortcomings in these pages, but I feel sure that if the student will read the foregoing, and will afterwaros study with care Lord Wolseley's " Decline and Fall of Napoleon " (chapters V. and VI.), also " The Story of Waterloo," by Colonel H. D. Hutchinson, both inexpensive works— and if he really means to pursue Military History, let him purchase for himself " The Operations of War," by Sir Edward Hamley, in the latter of which he will find a vast deal of military lore with its maps of many campaigns—he will find Military History both interesting and entertaining, and well worth the time and trouble that he spends upon it. I would recommend him to read the instructive works of the late Colonel Henderson, particularly "Stonewall Jackson," "The Battle of Spicheren," and "The Campaign of Fredericksburg," also "The Retreat from Moscow and Passage of the Beresina," by Colonel Turner, C.B.

I would also advise him to keep himself up to date by reading the Service Magazines and the articles in the weekly military papers.

In conclusion, I would quote Napoleon's own words, spoken at St. Helena, on the anniversary of the Battle of Waterloo—

"Incomprehensible day!" he said, sadly, "*concurrence of unheard-of fatalities*! .   . Grouchy! Ney!   . . .   D'Erlon!   . . . .   There was nothing but ill luck!   Ah! poor France!   . . . ." And he covered his eyes with his hand. "And, however," said he, "everything that depended on skill had been accomplished!   . . .   *Everything only failed when everything had succeeded*! . . . ." Again, he said, on the same subject, "Singular campaign, where, in less than one week, I saw three times slip from my hands the certain triumph of France and the crowning of my destiny.   But for the desertion of a traitor*, I should have annihilated the enemy in opening the

*General Bourmont, who was leading the advance of Gerard's Corps on the 15th June.

campaign. I should have overwhelmed them at Ligny, if my left had done its duty. I should have overwhelmed them at Waterloo, if my right had not failed me. . . . Singular defeat, where, in spite of the most horrible catastrophe, the glory of the vanquished has not suffered, nor that of the conqueror increased ; the memory of one will survive its destruction ; the memory of the other will perhaps bury itself in its triumph !"

Let the student consider for himself the truths and untruths contained in these words

NOTES AND APPENDIX.

I have included in this small book the Duke of Wellington's despatch after the Battles of Quatre-Bras and Waterloo. This despatch, written at Brussels the day after Waterloo, is addressed to Earl Bathurst; and also his despatch of same date, which was an addenda to the previous one.

The few notes I have added on these despatches may, I hope, prove interesting.

THE DUKE OF WELLINGTON'S DESPATCH.

To EARL BATHURST.

Waterloo, 19th June, 1815.

"Buonaparte, having collected the 1st, 2nd, 3rd, 4th, and 6th Corps of the French army, and the Imperial Guards, and nearly all the cavalry, on the Sambre, and between that river and the Meuse, between the 10th and 14th of the month, advanced on the 15th and attacked the Prussian posts at THUIN and LOBBES(1), on the SAMBRE, at daylight in the morning.

"I did not hear of these events till in the evening

of the 15th(2); and I immeaiately ordered the troops
to prepare to march, and afterwards to march to their
left, as soon as I had intelligence from other quarters
to prove that the enemy's movement upon CHARLEROI
was the real attack. The enemy drove the Prussian
posts from the SAMBRE on that day; and General
Ziethen, who commanded the corps which had been
at CHARLEROI, retired upon FLEURUS; and Marshal
Prince Blücher concentrated the Prussian army upon
SOMBREF, holding the villages in front of his position
of ST. AMAND and LIGNY.

" The enemy continued his march along the road
from CHARLEROI towards BRUXELLES, and, on the
same evening, the 15th, attacked a brigade of the
army of the Netherlands, under the Prince de Weimar,
posted at FRASNE, and forced it back to the farmhouse, on the same road, called LES QUATRE-BRAS(3).

" The Prince of Orange immediately reinforced this
brigade with another of the same division, under
General Perponcher(4), and, in the morning early,
regained part of the ground which had been lost, so
as to have command of the communication leading
from NIVELLES and BRUXELLES with Marshal
Blücher's position.

" In the meantime, I had directed the whole army
to march upon Les Quatre-Bras; and the 5th
Division(5), under Lieutenant-General Sir T. Picton,
arrived at about half-past two in the day, followed by

the corps of troops, under the Duke of Brunswick,
and afterwards by the contingent of NASSAU.   At
this time the enemy commenced an attack upon
Prince Blücher with his whole force, excepting the
1st and 2nd Corps(6), and a corps of cavalry under
General Kellermann, with which he attacked our post
at Les Quatre-Bras.

" The Prussian army maintained their position, with
their usual gallantry and perseverance, against a great
disparity of numbers, as the 4th Corps of their army,
under General Bülow(7), had not joined; and
I was not able to assist them as I wished(8), as I was
attacked myself, and the troops, the cavalry in
particular, which had a long distance to march, had
not arrived. We maintained our position also, and
completely defeated and repulsed all the enemy's
attempts to get possession of it.   The enemy
repeatedly attacked us with a large body of infantry
and cavalry, supported by a numerous and powerful
artillery.   He made several charges with the cavalry
upon our infantry, but all were repulsed in the
steadiest manner.

" In this affair, H.R.H. the Prince of Orange, the
Duke of Brunswick, and Lieutenant-General Sir T.
Picton, and Major-Generals Sir J. Kempt and Sir
Denis Pack, who were engaged from the commence-
ment of the enemy's attack, highly distinguished
themselves, as well as Lieutenant-General C. Baron

Alten, Major-General Sir C. Halkett, Lieutenant-General Cooke, and Major-Generals Maitland and Byng, as they successively arrived. The troops of the 5th Division, and those of the Brunswick Corps, were long and severely engaged, and conducted themselves with the utmost gallantry. I must particularly mention the 28th, 42nd, 79th, and 92nd Regiments and the battalion of Hanoverians.

" Our loss was great, as your Lordship will perceive by the enclosed return, and I have particularly to regret H.S.H. the Duke of Brunswick(9), who fell fighting gallantly at the head of his troops.

" Although Marshal Blücher had maintained his position at SOMBREF, he still found himself much weakened by the severity of the contest in which he had been engaged, and, as the 4th Corps had not arrived, he determined to fall back and to concentrate his army upon WAVRE ; and he marched in the night, after the action was over. This movement of the marshal rendered necessary a corresponding one upon my part ; and I retired from the farm of Quatre-Bras upon GENAPPE, and thence upon WATERLOO, the next morning, the 17th, at 10 o'clock.

" The enemy made no effort(10) to pursue Marshal Blücher. On the contrary, a patrole, which I sent to Sombref in the morning, found all quiet ; and the enemy's vedettes fell back as the patrole advanced. Neither did he attempt to molest our march to the rear(11), although made in the middle of the day, excepting by following, with a large body of cavalry brought from his right, the cavalry under the Earl of Uxbridge.

" This gave Lord Uxbridge an opportunity of charging them with the 1st Life Guards, upon their *débouché* from the village of Genappe, upon which occasion his Lordship has declared himself to be well satisfied with that regiment.

" The position(12) which I took up in front of Waterloo crossed the high roads from CHARLEROI and NIVELLES, and had its right thrown back to a ravine near MERKE BRAINE, which was occupied, and its left extended to a height above the hamlet TER LA HAYE, which was likewise occupied. In front of the right centre, and near the NIVELLES road, we occupied the house and gardens of Hougoumont, which covered the return of that flank ; and in front of the left centre we occupied the farm of LA HAYE SAINTE. By our left we communicated with Marshal Prince Blücher at WAVRE, through OHAIN ; and the Marshal had promised me that, in case we should be attacked, he would support me with one or more corps as might be necessary.

" The enemy collected his army, with the exception of the 3rd Corps, which had been sent to observe Marshal Blücher, on a range of heights in our front, in the course of the night of the 17th and yesterday morning, and at about 10 o'clock(13) he commenced a furious attack upon our post at Hougoumont.

" I had occupied that post with a detachment from General Byng's Brigade of Guards, which was in position in its rear; and it was for some time under command of Lieutenant-Colonel Macdonell(14), and afterwards of Colonel Home ; and I am happy to add that it was maintained throughout the day with the utmost gallantry by these brave troops, notwithstanding the repeated efforts of large bodies of the enemy to obtain possession of it. This attack upon the right of our centre was accompanied by a very heavy cannonade upon our whole line, which was destined to support the repeated attacks of cavalry and infantry, occasionally mixed, but sometimes separate, which were made upon it. In one of these the enemy carried the farmhouse of LA HAYE SAINTE(15), as the detachment of the light battalion of the German Legion, which occupied it, had expended all its ammunition ; and the enemy occupied the only communication there was with them.

" The enemy repeatedly charged our infantry with his cavalry(16), but these attacks were uniformly unsuccessful, and they afforded opportunities to our cavalry to charge, in one of which Lord E. Somerset's brigade, consisting of the Life Guards, the Royal Horse Guards, and 1st Dragoon Guards, highly distinguished themselves, as did that of Major-General

W. Ponsonby, having taken many prisoners and an eagle.

"These attacks were repeated till about seven in the evening, when the enemy made a desperate effort with cavalry and infantry, supported by the fire of artillery, to force our left centre, near the farm of LA HAYE SAINTE, which, after a severe contest, was defeated ; and, having observed that the troops retired from this attack in great confusion, and ʰthat the march of General Bülow's Corps, by Frischermont, upon Planchenois and La Belle Alliance, had begun to take effect, and as I could perceive the fire of his cannon, and as Marshal Prince Blücher had joined in person with a corps(17) of his army to the left of our line by OHAIN, I determined to attack the enemy(18), and immediately advanced the whole line of infantry, supported by the cavalry and artillery. The attack succeeded in every point ; the enemy was forced from his positions on the heights, and fled in the utmost confusion, leaving behind him, as far as I could judge, 150 pieces of cannon, with their ammunition, which fell into our hands.

"I continued the pursuit till long after dark(19), and then discontinued it, only on account of the fatigue of our troops, who had been engaged during twelve hours, and because I found myself on the same road with Marshal Blücher, who assured me of his intention to follow the enemy throughout the night.

He has sent me word this morning that he had taken 60 pieces of cannon belonging to the Imperial Guard, and several carriages, baggage, etc., belonging to Buonaparte, in Genappe.

" I propose to move this morning upon Nivelles, and not to discontinue my operations.

" Your Lordship will observe that such a desperate action could not be fought, and such advantages could not be gained, without great loss; and I am sorry to add that ours has been immense. In Lieutenant-General Sir T. Picton, His Majesty has sustained the loss of an officer who has frequently distinguished himself in his service; and he fell gloriously leading his division to a charge with bayonets, by which one of the most serious attacks made by the enemy on our position was repulsed. The Earl of Uxbridge, after having successfully got through this arduous day, received a wound by almost the last shot fired, which will, I am afraid, deprive His Majesty for some time of his services. His Royal Highness the Prince of Orange distinguished himself by his gallantry and conduct, till he received a wound from a musket ball through the shoulder, which obliged him to quit the field. It gives me the greatest satisfaction to assure your Lordship that the Army never, upon any occasion, conducted itself better. The division of Guards, under Lieutenant-General Cooke, who is severely wounded, Major-General Maitland, and

Major-General Byng, set an example which was followed by all ; and there is no officer nor description of troops that did not behave well.

" I must, however, particularly mention, for His Royal Highness's approbation, Lieutenant-General Sir H. Clinton, Major-General Adam, Lieutenant-General C. Baron Alten (severely wounded), Major-General Sir C. Halkett (severely wounded), Colonel Ompteda, Colonel Mitchell (commanding a brigade of the 4th Division), Major-Generals Sir J. Kempt and Sir D. Pack, Major-General Lambert, Major-General Lord E. Somerset, Major-General Sir W. Ponsonby, Major-General Sir C. Grant, Major-General Sir H. Vivian, Major-General Sir J. O. Vandeleur, and Major-General Count Dornberg.

" I am also particularly indebted to General Lord Hill for his assistance and conduct upon this, as upon all former occasions. The artillery and engineer departments were conducted, much to my satisfaction, by Colonel Sir G. Wood and Colonel Smyth ; and I had every reason to be satisfied with the conduct of the Adjutant-General, Major-General Barnes, who was wounded, and of the Quartermaster-General, Colonel De Lancey, who was killed by a cannon shot in the middle of the action. This officer is a serious loss to His Majesty's Service, and to me at this moment.

" I was likewise much indebted to the assistance of

Lieutenant-Colonel Lord FitzRoy Somerset, who was severely wounded, and of the officers composing my personal staff(20), who have suffered severely in this action. Lieutenant-Colonel the Hon. Sir A. Gordon, who has died of his wounds, was a most promising officer, and is a serious loss to His Majesty's Service.

" General Krüse, of the Nassau Service, likewise conducted himself much to my satisfaction ; as did General Trip, commanding the heavy brigade of cavalry, and General Vanhope, commanding a brigade of infantry in the service of the King of the Netherlands.

" General Pozzo di Borgo, General Baron Vincent, General Müffling, and General Alava, were in the field during the action, and rendered me every assistance in their power. Baron Vincent is wounded, but I hope not severely ; and General Pozzo di Borgo received a contusion.

" I should not do justice(21) to my own feelings or to Marshal Blücher and the Prussian Army, if I did not attribute the successful result of this arduous day to the cordial and timely assistance I received from them. The operation of General Bülow upon the enemy's flank was a decisive one ; and even if I had not found myself in a situation to make the attack, which produced the final result, it would have forced the enemy to retire if his attacks should have failed, and would have prevented him from taking advantage of them if they should unfortunately have succeeded.

"Since writing the above, I have received a report that Major-General Sir W. Ponsonby is killed; and in announcing this intelligence to your Lordship I have to add the expression of my grief for the fate of an officer who had already rendered very brilliant and important services, and was an ornament to his profession.

"I send with this despatch three eagles, taken by the troops in this action, which Major Percy will have the honour of laying at the feet of His Royal Highness. I beg leave to recommend him to your Lordship's protection."

———

To Earl Bathurst,

Bruxelles, 19th June, 1815.

"I have to inform your Lordship, in addition to my despatch of this morning, that we have already got here 5,000 prisoners, taken in the action of yesterday, and that there are about 2,000 more coming in to-morrow. There will probably be many more. Amongst the prisoners are the Comte de Lobau(22), who commanded the 6th Corps, and General Cambrone, who commanded a division of the Guards. I propose to send the whole to England, by Ostend."

NOTES ON THE DUKE OF WELLINGTON'S DESPATCH.

NOTE 1.—Thuin, a town in Hainault, on the river Sambre (see map); Lobbes, a village 2 miles north-west of Thuin.

NOTE 2.—The Prince of Orange, who came in to dine with the Duke at 3 p.m., from Braine-le-Comte, previous to the famous ball given by the Duchess of Richmond, was the first to inform the Duke of the French attack. The news was shortly afterwards corroborated by General Müffling, the Prussian Commissioner at the British headquarters, the mounted orderly sent by Ziethen early in the day having lost his way.

NOTE 3.—Les Quatre-Bras—the four arms—where the four roads going to Brussels in the north, Charleroi in the south, Nevilles to the west, and Namur to the east, meet.

NOTE 4.—General Perponcher commanded the Dutch-Belgians.

NOTE 5.—The famous 5th Division, commanded by Lieutenant-General Sir Thomas Picton, consisted of the 8th and 9th British Brigades. The 8th Brigade was under the command of Major-General Sir J. Kempt, and was made up of the following battalions: —28th Regiment, 32nd Regiment, 79th Regiment, 95th Regiment.

The 9th Brigade was commanded by Major-General Sir Denis Pack, and was made up of the following battalions :—1st Regiment (3rd Battalion disbanded shortly afterwards), 42nd Regiment, 44th Regiment, and 92nd Regiment.

NOTE 6.—The Duke was of the opinion that both the corps of Reille and D'Erlon were opposed to him at Quatre-Bras.   As we know D'Erlon was moving aimlessly about between the two battlefields of Ligny and Quatre-Bras, and Girard's division of Reille's Corps was deflected to the right to watch the Prussians.   So thus, instead of there being two corps, *i.e.*, eight divisions, there were only three divisions opposed to the Duke at Quatre-Bras.   "So severe had been the struggle at Quatre-Bras, that in his great despatch on the Waterloo Campaign Wellington officially reports that he had been attacked by the combined corps of Reille and D'Erlon (eight divisions), a misstatement, doubtless due to the evidence of prisoners as to the corps designed for the attack, and to the report of the Prince of Orange, who formed the same opinion ; but, considering the hand that wrote it, a magnificent testimony to the fighting efficiency of the three French divisions which in fact assailed him."—(General F. Maurice).

NOTE 7.—General Bülow was, as we have seen, at Liege on the 14th June, and had not sufficiently understood the urgency of the case in the order sent him by Gneisenau, the chief of the Prussian Staff, and thus was not moving rapidly enough to be present at Ligny on the 16th.

NOTE 8.—Wellington, it will be remembered, when he rode over to see Blücher, whom he met at a windmill, between Ligny and Brye, promised to come to Blücher's assistance at 4 p.m., *if not seriously attacked himself.*

NOTE 9.—To the Duke of Brunswick, Lord Byron devotes one of his magnificent stanzas in Childe Harold's Pilgrimage, which ends up with—

> " He rush'd into the field, and,
> Foremost fighting, fell."

NOTE 10.—The student will recollect Grouchy's vain attempt to get instructions from Napoleon, to pursue the Prussians, it not being till 1 p.m. on the 17th June that he received verbal orders, and only reached Gembloux at 9 p.m., being delayed by the torrents of rain and the heavy state of the roads. The Prussians in the meantime had retired on Wavre.

NOTE 11.—" The force collected by Wellington at Quatre-Bras, amounting to 45,000 men, began to fall back on Mont St. Jean about 10 a.m. on the 17th. The movement was leisurely and admirably carried out under the Duke's personal direction, and by the time that Ney actually began to move against him

Wellington's cavalry alone remained on the position.
By 2 p.m. the pursuit was retarded by the same
torrential rain that had burst upon Grouchy's column
as he was setting out for Gembloux.   With the
exception of an insignificant skirmish at Genappe, and
such artillery fire as the French could bring to bear
upon our retreating cavalry, nothing of interest
marked this movement upon Mont St. Jean."—(Lord
Wolseley).

NOTE 12.—The student should take special notice
of the Duke's description of his position at Waterloo.

" The chateau and grounds of Hougonmont on the
right, the farm of La Haie Sainte in the centre, and
the hamlets of Papelotte, La Haye, and Smohain on
the left, were held as advancing posts by the British."
—(Colonel Hutchinson).

NOTE 13.—" The hour at which Waterloo began,
though there were 150,000 actors in the great tragedy,
was long a matter of dispute.   The Duke puts it at
10 o'clock, General Alava says 11.30, and Napoleon
and Drouet say 12 o'clock, and Ney 1 o'clock.   Lord
Hill may be credited with having settled this minute
question of fact.   He took two watches with him
into the fight, one a stop-watch, and he marked with
it the sound of the first shot fired, and that evidence is
now accepted as proving that the first flash of red
flame which marked the opening of the world-shaking
tragedy of Waterloo took place at exactly ten minutes

to twelve."—" Deeds that won the Empire," by the
Rev. W. H. Fitchett.

NOTE 14.—Lieutenant-Colonel Macdonnell judged
by Wellington to be the bravest soldier at Waterloo.
" A patriotic Briton bequeathed £500 (to be given) to
the bravest soldier at Waterloo, the Duke of
Wellington to be the judge. The Duke named
Macdonnell, who handed the money to the sergeant
who was his comrade in the struggle at the gate of
Hougoumont."—" Deeds that won the Empire."

NOTE 15.—" There is much discrepancy as to the
hour when La Haye Sainte was captured. General
Kennedy, on the English side, and Colonel Heymés,
Ney's aide-de-camp, on that of the French, put the
hour at 6 p.m.—that is, towards the end of the period
of the French cavalry charges. Others put it as early
as 4 p.m. There is, however, one piece of evidence
about which there can be little dispute : it is the copy
of a letter from Lieutenant Graeme, of the Hanoverian
Service, who took part in the defence of that place, a
letter which has appeared in Siborne's recently-
published ' Waterloo Letters ' (p. 409). In it he
mentions that when he was retreating from La Haye
Sainte ' all the army was formed in squares.' It is
clear, therefore, that the place fell during the period
of the cavalry charges. The whole story of the
defence and its details shows that it must have been
towards evening that the French carried it. Owing

to the length of the struggle for its possession, and
the neglect to provide a postern, the defenders were
at last left without any ammunition.   The denseness
of the fog and smoke prevented any but those who
were on the spot from seeing what was going on
there ; and, taking all the evidence we have on this
point, I am led to think that 6 p.m. must have been
about the hour when La Haye Sainte fell.   In fact,
the French took advantage of the circumstance that
their cavalry were at the moment occupying the
attention of Wellington and his army to renew and
push home their direct attack upon this rather isolated
outpost.   Having once carried it, they filled it with
sharpshooters.   These made a neighbouring knoll
untenable, and enabled the French artillery to bring
so heavy a fire upon a portion of the English position
as to compel a square, composed of the 30th and 73rd
Regiments, to withdraw to a bank in rear, more or
less in confusion.   At the same moment some Brunswickers near this spot were driven back, and the
consequence was a dangerous gap in the line of battle.
It was a critical moment, and if fresh French troops
could have been immediately thrown into the gap it
is practically certain that the English front must have
been broken.   Wellington met the danger with
admirable coolness and skill.   The arrival, just at this
juncture, of one of Ziethen's brigades on his left
released Vivian's and Vandeleur's brigades of horse-

nen, and they were at once thrown into the gap. By the time that Napoleon was able to turn his attention from the Prussian attack at Planchenoit to this final attack upon the British, who stood between him and Brussels, Wellington had thoroughly reformed his fighting line, and Ziethen was within close supporting distance of him, while Pirch was closing up in support of Bülow for a renewed attack on Napoleon's right." —(Lord Wolseley).

NOTE 16.—The magnificent and self-sacrificing charges of the British cavalry, which bore excellent fruit, should be taken note of by the student ; also of the thirteen cavalry charges, lasting three hours, on the part of the French, which bore no fruit whatever, only resulting in the annihilation of this body of superb horsemen.

NOTE 17.—Ziethen's Corps.

NOTE 18.—" Wellington at once sent the cavalry brigades of Vivian and Vandeleur in pursuit. Almost at the same moment the main body of Zeithen's Corps arrived, forcing itself in between the right of D'Erlon in his attack on the English left and the left of Lobau's Corps in its contest with the Prussians, under Bülow. Zeithen thus turned both those French corps. The Duke seized the moment to order the general advance of his whole line. Despite the heroic efforts made by many splendid French soldiers, the rout soon became a mere *sauve-qui-peut*."—(Lord Wolseley).

NOTE 19.—" There was nothing now to do but to arrange for the pursuit. This the English were too exhausted to take part in, but by the Prussians it was undertaken with such indefatigable energy that by daylight the next morning some of their cavalry had reached Gosselies, twenty miles from the scene of the fight. Napoleon, himself flying all night, reached Charleroi at six in the morning. Here the fugitives were already pouring across the bridges, but out of the 72,000 marshalled for the fight at Waterloo barely 40,000 re-crossed the Sambre, and they carried with them only 27 guns out of the 240 they had taken into action. The loss to the Allies was upwards of 22,000 in killed and wounded, and of this total the Prussians' share was just 7,000."—Colonel H. D. Hutchinson.

NOTE 20.—The student should read the following in conjunction with the previous note :—" Here it was arranged that the Prussians, who had fallen in upon the same road with the English, should continue the pursuit. For, though the Duke made arrangements to support them with part of his troops, these proved to be so completely exhausted by the fatigues of battle, that they could not go on. A halt was, therefore, ordered mid-way between Rossomme and Genappes. From that point the Duke rode slowly home, in clear moonlight, and alone. Scarcely one of his old companions through the War of the Peninsular remained to cheer him with his congratulations.

Colonel De Lancy, his quartermaster-general, had received a mortal wound; Major-General Barnes, his adjutant general, was wounded also; Lieutenant-Colonel FitzRoy Somerset, his faithful and attached military secretary, had lost an arm, and been carried to Brussels. Of his aides-de-camp, two, Colonel the Hon. Alexander Gordon and Lieutenant-Colonel Canning, were both struck down. The latter died on the spot; the former only survived to learn from the chief whom he had long served and dearly loved, that the battle was won. Indeed, the losses that day to England, and to the best blood of England, were terrible. Lord Uxbridge, struck by one of the last shots fired, suffered the amputation of a limb. Picton, the hero of a hundred fights, went whither his glory could not follow him. But it would be vain to attempt to particularise, one by one, the brave who purchased with their blood that day a renown which can never perish. The authentic lists of killed and wounded showed a grand total, on the side of the Allies, of 23,185. Out of this enormous multitude the English alone lost 11,678; the Netherlanders, 3,178; the Brunswickers, 687; the troops of Nassau, 643; the Prussians, 6,999. The loss of the French is not quite so easily determined. According to Colonel Charras it amounted to 31,000 or 32,000. Napoleon reckons it at 23,600 only; of these 7,000 were prisoners. If we include the casualties which befel in the pursuit, it

E

was probably 40,000 at the least."—" Gleig's Life of Wellington."

NOTE 21.—Observe that the Duke gives the fullest credit to the Prussians for the part they played in the great battle.

NOTE 22.—" Meantime, Lobau was bravely maintaining an unequal fight amid the burning ruins of Plancenoit, and it was not till some time after the overthrow of the guard, that, yielding to the ever-increasing pressure in front, he was at last obliged to abandon the village to the victorious Prussians."— Colonel H. D. Hutchinson.